DEDICATION

To my sweet Thomas William,

I have so many words that I want to say to you and although I feel like in the comfort of darkness, with our heads on a pillow face to face we have the best conversations, there's a lot that is too hard to vocalize when your eyes are sparkling at me. Even on my worst days, which unfortunately can come all too often during a global pandemic- you not only pick my pieces up for me but you re-build them in a way I'd never thought to... you build me up with love that I find so hard to understand because I've never loved myself the way that you do. You have taught me what it means to treat myself with care, to be patient with myself while I heal, to believe in myself no matter what I do. You showed me how good it feels to stand at the stove stirring dinner, when a pair of hairy arms wrap around my abdomen and pull me in close just to whisper that you love me and call me "your little chef" What a beautiful experience it is to be on the receiving end of what a thoughtful, compassionate, patient, understanding, hilarious, and handsome human being you are. I am now and forever will be baffled how someone so perfect for me exists, every time that we make the same terrible jokes, we sink the same beer pong cup, we mock Alora's accents together, yell at the TV every time the Yankees lose, and order the same thing at every restaurant we go to. You are my best friend, and I can't wait to see you grow into the grumpiest, grouchiest, old man on earth. I am so grateful that you took a chance on me, and I want to say that I will never stop trying to be what you deserve in a woman. Thank you for loving me.

PREFACE

I just want to preface this whole thing by saying that this is a lot of poetry that tells small stories about pieces of my life. Some it is very direct and some not so much, for those of you in my family, I'm sorry for some of what is to come, and if it seems that things are a little out of order, that's because in my life they occur the same way. Healing is a not a straight path, and neither is destruction. On the same days that I feel overwhelmed with love, are sometimes the days I find it hardest just to get up out of bed. Writing this knowing that it could reach others- It's one way for me to heal and has been so therapeutic just allowing myself to say whatever it is that I wanted to say, rather than holding back and worrying about what people would think of me. I have taken the blame and the responsibility for many things that have been done to me and I'm done with that now. This book does not name any names, but it does recall a handful of traumatic events that I've never spoken about until now, because there is no reason that I should have to feel shame over choices that I did not personally make. I just want to say thank you to my many wonderful, supportive friends who have helped me through this past year and a half of my life. Things have been a lot harder than most know, and I have been searching for ways to feel like who I used to be, but she is gone and that's OKAY. For all of you reading this who have been through similar things, I am so sorry. I am so sorry if nobody believed you, if someone shamed you, if you've been made to feel like a person barely existing inside of shell, if you had to get up and go to work the next day, if you couldn't stomach looking yourself in the mirror, if for a few days you couldn't even hold your own child because you couldn't remember how to be a mother. I'm sorry if you've even been entered without your consent. I'm sorry if you have even been in a relationship so toxic it makes you lose your identity, I'm sorry if nothing you've ever done has been enough. You are enough for me, and I hope that I am enough for you. We matter no matter who tells us otherwise, no matter your size, your race, your orientation, your interests, your experience, your political affiliation. You matter.

death grip

I could walk away

Everything could change today

If I could just walk away

I wish you would stop pulling so hard

I'm trying to walk away

Please let go of my shirt now

It's time for me to walk away

Your screams are so loud, they're deafening

Maybe you're right, it's selfish to walk away

I'm so tired, I'm desperate, yearning for change

Oh. You're leaving?

You can't stand me?

You're walking the fuck away?

I wonder what it would be like

If you would have just

Let

Me

Walk

Away

sour

the toxic taste of

you

is haunting me

I just want the

bitterness to end

let go

giving up is bravery

letting go is strength

weakness is not defined

by your ability to walk away

knowing when "enough is enough"

will never lead your heart astray

give yourself the chance

to collect your pride and move along

You deserve more, and you will find it

tomorrow is another fucking day.

ghost in plain sight

You're nothing but a memory

watching you like a series of flashes

a well depicted collection of

"way back when's"

way back when

is loosely translated to

"when I had those feelings"

"when we spent time together"

"when I used to love you"

who knew then?

we were making

"way back when's"

eraser crumbs

and it's funny how most days

I go on without ever

thinking of your face

but it's funny how most days

I can't stop from wishing

that I never even knew your name

Mickeys bar

I saw your eyes glimmer

in the lights from this

Christmas tree

and it reminded me

of the first time I saw you

under all those strobe lights

in the dark and musky dive bar

playing along to some reggae

with your hat on backwards

and your eyes forward

in my direction

you didn't notice me

but I noticed you.

I saw your eyes glimmer

in the lights from the ceiling

and I knew right then

that I needed to know you.

how do I name a poem with only one line?

I just want to fucking matter

I trusted you.

You were her.

In every dark place

You were her.

In every empty space

You were her.

On every tough day

You were her...

And I trusted you.

I told you no

And you ignored it.

I said I couldn't

And you said I'm boring.

You made me believe that

In order to be me

I had to be like you

But you fucking deceived me

When you climbed up on top

And you held my head down

You locked my legs open

And you looked at the ground

Because this wasn't for you

And it wasn't for me

This was for him

And his sick fucking fantasies

What baffles me most

Is the lack of regard

For what would be left

When I pulled myself up

Why didn't you wonder

How I would feel

Or ever consider

If I would be able to deal

With this kind of trauma

So close to the other

If my heart could survive this

If my mind would recover

And when I stood myself up

When I got up from that place

And I looked in the mirror

I didnt remember my face

Because I wasn't the same woman

From just that same morning

I was someone new, someone older

Someone wiser, and someone used

Someone broken, someone tired

Someone hurting, and someone confused

I was none of the things

That I'd been working so hard for

Because all of that disappeared

The moment he opened my front door

And now I cant stand

to push past the shame

I am nothing

I am no-one

I will never be the same.

Because you're selfish

 And you used me.

And we will never ever be the same.

lost

And ever since that day

Who the fuck am I?

euphemism

I wish there were a way to say no

Without ever parting my lips

choking

It wells up in my throat

and I can't seem to make it move

I'm choking

on my behalf

swallowing my pride

it tastes just like defeat

you are her

open your ears

you are her

open your eyes

you are her

open your mind

you are her

open your heart

you are her

even when you aren't her

she is her

never underestimate

how hard it is

to be her

Just incase I don't see you when you get home

remember that I love you

and just incase I don't talk to you during lunch break

please remember that I love you

just incase I miss you when we're passing in the hallway

I need you to know how much I love you

and just incase it feels empty when we're laying in bed together

it's keeping me awake, dreaming about my love for you

and if you're ever hurt, or lost, or full of doubt

take my love and heal yourself

I'll count the pieces that I have left

alongside the days since you've been gone

and if you add them all up

maybe then I'll be enough

songbird

pieces of a melody

a far-off flightless tune

a beautifully sung serenade

to the rhythm of

another lonely you

stifled

every time you told me to be quiet

i learned to shut up no matter what

every time you told me that it didn't matter

i learned not to take myself seriously

every time you told me that I was being dramatic

i learned to minimize my trauma

every time you put your hands on me

i learned that hands will find their way

and every time that you ignored me

i learned that it doesn't matter how loud i scream

so i might as well just be quiet.

fake I.d.

Between my thighs

is like a hidden night club

meant to enter

only by use of a password

or spoken invitation

so why,

if I kept the location a secret

would you barge in

without my permission

between my thighs

is a night club

full of people

I never asked to be there

stagnant

I can't make myself move

from this couch

from this bed

from this shower

from this chair

from this place in my life

empty

My pieces could never make you whole

But I'm incomplete without them

exhausted

I'm

    So

        Tired

I wish that the world understood

What it's like to be broken

Without all the mockery

Without any of the shame

With just an ounce of understanding

And a lot less victim blame

illuminati on

have you ever watched a candle fill a room

bursting with light, smell, warmth

there's nothing more beautiful about a candle

than the reflection of a flame in a nearby window

And there's nothing more captivating than you

Embodying the sweet aroma

Emanating all that heat

Ember blazon with illumination

Reflecting all my favorite parts of me

comfort me

days like these

i need the comfort of your touch

i need a warm caress, a brush

i need the electricity of our skin

i need the sparks that fly from her to him

i need a hand to cup my chubby chin

i need unexpected adventure on a whim

on days like these

i need you

I can't be poetic right now

The physical parts of what happened aren't even what hurt me the most.

As awful as this may sound, they didn't batter me, they didn't have to because I didn't fight back,
but the memories of how it felt faded quickly enough to heal.

What hurt me the most is what this did to my head, to my heart, to who I am, and who I was becoming
as a person?

I have spent the past 365 days telling myself that this was my fault.

I shouldn't have to recover my mind, my body, and my heart.

I shouldn't have to reclaim myself as a piece of land I fought to own.

you

You make me feel like every star in the sky

a void to fill

I'm so sorry that I was never enough for you

But I'm sorrier that I've never been enough for me

Or I would have known that I was too good for you

And I would have realized that you were nothing

anew

And he made her feel confidence

Oozing from her pores

The very pores from the body

That just that same morning

Spoke down to her only reflection

But she had never felt love

In the way that he showed it

He made her feel like poetry

And not the type that you write

To overcome your obstacles

But the type that makes you feel

A sun-kissed warmth in an open field

Like effervescence of a handful

Of the finest fresh picked daisies

Wild

insomniac

and I can't seem to sleep

with thoughts of you

dancing in my memory

I don't want to wake up

and find your space empty

I called out to you

I called out your name

I called out to you

but it was too late

a sideways glance

a misread stance

the trouble with perception

the same thing today

just like all these yesterdays

how long will it be the same?

without a change of scenery

how long will it be before?

you just can't stand the sight of me

and I don't want to wake up

wondering

this one is about what it feels like to be in love with you

Walking backwards on the moon

Earth dancing with you

it's so hard to sleep at night

the tears

they well up anyway

and the dreams

they're uglier than I could ever convey

the feelings

are heavy

and the burden

is dreaded

but the love

is the same

the love

never fades

thank you for loving me

I've loved before,

sure

But I don't know

that I've ever been

in love

before now

I've ever been

shown love

until now

wrapped in blankets

and above our heads

you can plainly see

the clouds that have formed

filled with laughs and sincerity

and around our hearts

is the string that binds

a solitary drum beat

a force that intertwines

[plasma]

trying to embody the electricity in my skin

the sedated state of mind you put me in

the earth is not a cold dead place

and the one who taught me that, is you

like a faucet

It's easier when you're young.

It's easy to hold his hand, to kiss him goodbye

to walk away to a place where he no longer exists

it's all so easy when you're young.

Because now, he feels like a fixture

so in love with loving you

and then I fell.

I fell from the earth,

I fell from the sky,

I fell from below

I fell from up high

I fell in a way,

      that was old

            but felt new

I fell in a way,

      that led me

            right to you.

And it's easier to fall asleep when our hands are intertwined

hunnybee

The place he where he stands is warm,

and in this case, I'm not too fond of the chill.

The place where he lays is full,

and even with my body in his absence, it's empty still.

Because now he feels so permanent

and when he's gone the lights won't turn on

So instead, I lay alone in the dark

and learn the words to all his favorite songs

you make everything better

searching for ways to describe how you make my toes curl

my cheeks blushed, rosy with affirmation

the shivers down my spine, cliche but real

caressing my cheek, a soft press to warm flesh

loss of doubt in the moments you fill

inquisitive for every bit of who you are

walk me hand in hand through adventures amongst the stars

You make everything better.

climax

and then I fell.

without a whisper

nothing but a touch

warm lips pressed

say so much

wandering fingertips

trace my skin

gripping you tight

sliding it in.

bodies in rhythm

pulling you closer

how did I climax

before I knew who, you were

and from the moment I met you

everything has changed

my world turned upside down

in the most beautiful way.

and each time that you touch me

my whole body shakes

I'm tingling, I'm trembling

I can't feel my face

so tired of being so sad

Sadness

seeping sadness

sleeping through sadness

is harder than it sounds

the sounds of sadness are deafening

the sound of absolute silence

followed by complete chaos

everyone is just so fucking sad

valuables

Help me turn all the mirrors the other way

Take all these feelings and rip them away

How do I admit to myself?

How do I commit to myself?

How do I explain to myself?

That what you say is true

That who I am has VALUE

concrete

Don't take my picture

Take a fucking Xray

Because the woman inside of me

Is who the hell I want to be

That girl has come a long way

And she deserves better...

She deserves everything.

I feel

I can feel

I can

I feel

There are glistens on my fingertips

My once wiped tears

Those feelings I felt

Those tears that all fell

Those memories, that hell

How did I get here?

I can feel

I can

I feel

There is a pounding in my chest

My once broken heart

Those feelings I felt

Those tears that all fell

Those memories, that hell

How did I get here?

I can feel

I can

I feel

There is no air in my lungs

My once shallow breaths

Those feelings I felt

Those tears that all fell

Those memories, that hell

How did I get here?

I can't feel

I can't

My eyes are not leaking

My heart has stopped beating

My lungs have stopped breathing

My life has no meaning

And I have no feeling

How did I get here?

I don't want to be here.

the shadow in my corner

I had a brother, who became very sick, he did pass away when he was 6.

So though he was not physically a piece of my patch work,

I often found myself pretending he was there just so that I didn't have to feel so alone in my own version of broken.

I can recall so many instances as a kid when I would get myself into trouble and once I got sent to my room I would sit on my bed having full blown conversations with my very dead brother.

It's always been easier to talk to him though, because when you get to oversee both ends of a conversation it typically goes the way you would like it to,

as opposed to the screaming matches, I had grown so accustomed to.

yearning

The water is running

And my heart is yearning

Searching

For answers that can only be found on the shower floor

And they've washed away now

You let them go now

So I said goodbye now

I said goodbye, but just for now.

the best part of waking up

Your voice is so soothing

Like a fresh cup of well brewed coffee

on why I never left my toxic relationship

You told me every fucking day

said it in 15 different ways

you told me every fucking day

But I don't like change

so I still stayed.

because humans are fragile

How do we decide what parts of our life, are the parts that define us? How do we stumble through our proudest moments, and wade through the ever-flowing river of trauma, and decide what parts of which made us who we are today? Deciding whether a characteristic is just a characteristic, or a deafening flaw created by years of holding in the hurt of every empty needle, every covered-up bruise, every blood-stained blanket, and every empty kiss goodnight.

I think often, we don't decide these things ourselves, but rather someone close to us who has been front row seated for the destruction of our lives can eventually pull us aside and inform us that, that thing that we are doing is incredibly toxic. Not only toxic, but we have been doing this very toxic thing for a very long time, preceded by a laundry list of examples when we allowed this trait to ruin our own lives. Only then do we as people realize "oh this isn't supposed to be a part of who I am, but it is and I should probably figure out why."

I have spent a fair amount of my adult life being directed to my own toxicity and analyzing it obsessively to make myself a more tolerable person to be around. I find myself often looking for the words to describe an entire lifetime's worth of back story to anyone, when I need to explain WHY an event was so important to me, or a sentence struck so many chords, why a song gave me goosebumps, or why a whiff of another woman's perfume brought me to tears.

The events that occur throughout our time here, really do make us. They make us good people, they make us bad, and that is just the nitty gritty of it. We are eventually responsible for our response to events, but we can't expect someone to be strong all the time in response to terrible things.

That's how artists are born.

stargazer

She didn't know how possible it was

to rip the stars right from the night sky

to hold them in her hands

to see them shine

She was power

fueled by the fire

burning from within

in the center of the storm

brewed by no other witch

a spell, a look, a midnight muse

She had all the power

Power over you

touch me one more time

all I could feel was your touch,

your fingers glide across my naked skin

and all I could hear was your words,

the musings of a smitten man

and all I could sense was your love,

perfectly poured cups, of plentiful adoration

and all of it I must have made up,

the heart of a lonely girl, longing.

open up

Fast asleep,

I had a dream

of a picture-perfect ending.

My eyes held closed

and no one knows

just how alone you are

until they open up.

explanation, left behind

justification, tossed aside

I wish I never woke up.

once upon a fucking time

picture perfect

I deserve this

the hurt was worth it

I'm the real gift.

enough

Let me

Let me feel these good things

Let me

Let me see what you see in me

Let me

Let me understand how to feel worthy

Let me

Let me be her.

        Let me be him.

                Let me be you.

      Please, just let me.

    Let me be who I imagined I would be.

     Let me be enough for you.

glaucoma

It's getting harder for me to see, and I guess that's okay

I wish that everything could be as vivacious as it should be,

but I know that my mind remembers so vividly.

empty motivations

I have a heart that has been removed

You have a heart that's never been used

caught up in the technicalities

But i can say with certainty

that you have destroyed what was left of me.

sought out explanations

with endless determination

erratic interrogation

empty motivations

I found myself screaming

I found myself screaming for you

I found myself screaming at you

I found myself silent

I found your face

in the pictures

of every thing I've ever hated

I found your voice

in echoes surrounding

every time I've ever been mistreated

It's all about what we know

splinter becomes the open wound

a single thread is an unwound bloom

Speak easy...

In circles,

around

in treason,

we're bound

to walk freely

barely above ground.

adhd

Being the creative one, with a voice too loud to contain

makes it hard to be the one who suffers in silence most days.

unrealistic expectations

grab my hair and drag me across this dirty floor

pull me up by my ratty clothes

tell me what you've been waiting for

for something that isn't so disappointing

for someone who does more

tell me all the things I haven't done

as if I never knew.

Waste my time, like I've wasted yours

done so much, but it's never enough

as many times as you have let me go

I have always managed to stand back up

Invincible, for me

I stand, for you

the storm will rage

regardless of the face

but I carry on, because you need me

and I need me too.

tent

That's the fantasy, right? The perfect dream?

The one where you deflower me, and I'm too scared to scream?

It worked out in your favor really, because I couldn't understand you

you see, there was a vicious cycle in play here,

because your father assaulted you.

But now here I am, picture me only 8 years old.

I'm lying on my bedroom floor, and I'm staring at my Barney sheets

strewn through the air above me, draped with betrayal and misery

they concealed the thing that I most feared

and fear itself lived inside of you

and I watched my innocence drip from your fingertips...

as my future flashed, in my eyes blue

I think somehow, I knew right then, that from this day on I would never be okay.

But it wasn't just one day, or months, but years.

You held me down, you covered my mouth,

you yelled to our parents "we're coming right out"

I never had a chance, and nobody even knew

that because you had suffered, now I suffered too

why does this keep happening to me?

Here she is

she is soft, and she is young

She didn't know then that this wouldn't be the last time

It wouldn't be the last guy

it happens more than you know.

Just like any other thing,

some days it's harder to believe

It never feels like it was me

some days it's harder to breathe

it doesn't feel like I can see

To be a human

is a funny thing

split second decision made by you

lifetime of misery for me

sweet and sour bebe

I want a love story

As simple as a fortune cookie

I hear them talk

I am enough

I am too much

I am more

I am deserving

I deserved it

"she deserved it"

that's what they say

that's what they say about me now...

embers

If I could feel the embers

I would blow them

blow them all away

fingertips singed

skin so scorned

flesh that burns

watch you melt away

Invincible

Inspiration like a flower petal on the wind

infinite sorrow

the throbbing on the surface

is the least of my problems

so when I tilt my head back

and I pick up the bottle

I spiral down to my comfort zone,

drowning my infinite sorrow,

One sip at a time

without a care for tomorrow

My peace comes within sight,

reality is fading

Theres nothing more than you can do

Theres no way for you to save me

wholesome fun

I remember walks along the riverbank with you

I remember walks along the sand dunes

Far and wide, every walk of life with you

I had no idea which way to go,

but I knew that wherever it was I had to bring you too

The demons were always beside us,

shadows cast on the bad days

but no matter how far we walked,

sunset inevitably came.

aftermath

she isn't me

this girl in the mirror can't be me

her hair is disheveled

she looks lost and confused

below the reflection, where she can't see

blood drips to the floor

holes are ripped in her favorite jeans

HER hands won't stop shaking

she only has one shoe on her feet

she stumbled, then ran here

to face her own fears

that it happened anyway

even after she said no

maybe she should have said it louder

perhaps he didn't hear her

it had to be her own fault

that's what society had taught her

but staring at her broken reflection

none of that seemed to be real

because this was her body

and she owned it.

but he came inside of her

like this was the way, and she had showed him

he ran his intrusive fucking hands

up her thighs, and into her pants

fast asleep and skin so bare

i never said that he could touch me there

ranch and cold pizza

Blood. There's blood. There's so much blood.

   Brain matter garnished the forests trees, the sunrise laid light on the red painted leaves.

Loud. So loud. Nobody ever said it would be so loud.

   We danced circles in the moonlight, slow and calculated movements.

Empty. I'm empty. I never knew I could feel this empty.

   You sang to me the lullabies of a mad man masquerading

Hurt. This hurt. The blood is loud, and the emptiness hurts.

   Your soul I held in my hands, now set free into the riverbank

Lost. My eyes do not deceive me, beautiful rebellion, lost in your last breath.

Heavy. The bullets ricochet in my chest, from your skull.

Quiet. Choking down every word, wallowing in the absence of your wander.

Confused. How are we supposed to watch the sun set if you're not here?

Blood. There's blood. There's so much blood.

I drove with my eyes closed and no hands on the steering wheel today

I did it so I could feel closer to you.

to be a woman

Someone teach me how to be beautiful

I wasn't born with it, like I wish I had been

manic

You should have seen me last week

I wrote a romance novel,

I drew a picture of your face,

I took a million photographs,

I spent my nights baking cakes,

I organized my clothes by color,

I polished all of the furniture.

You should have been here last week

I was a completely different person.

see me

I'm not the face, nor the body, that I used to be.

I know that there is more to me,

but It's so hard to believe,

when all of beauty is perception

and I can't quite see how you perceive me.

giving up

Departure from these indentations

means I must find a new way

to make things stay.

There is

                          Never

Pieces

                          Enough

   of

                          of

you

                          you

in

                          in

everything

                          my

that

                          Immediate

I

                          Surroundings.

see.

You are you.

         You are every clean set of sheets

         You are the puddles splashing under my feet

         You are everything in between

         You are the world, in every good dream

         You are every breath I take, of fresh air

         You are the sun.

         You are the moon.

         You are beauty.

And you are me.

I
R
I
D
E
S
C
A
N
T...

want to gaze into these beams of light
need to see something prophetic
need to believe, the story that the morning sun sings
never told my tales, sunrise schematics in my dreams
so many hills to climb, if I'm ever going to catch the
morning rain

Fixation on the new horizon
Blooming curiosity in early morning

please, just stay with me

Can I stay?

right here, like a wildflower in the meadows of your silk sheets?

Can I stay?

here with you, hours passing by like shooting stars, lost in the beauty of imagination?

Can I stay?

right here, painting gold trimmed memories in the moonlight.

Can I stay?

here with you, swirled together like cream and a fresh cup of coffee?

Can I stay so that I know, no matter when you leave,

when you come back, you'll always be coming back for me?

Will you stay?

   Will you stay for me?

      Will you be what's left of me?

        Will you ask me if I'll stay?

      just this once, just for today?

Please just stay with me.

mid-sized sedan

I am not the curves of the body that make your heart skip beats

but I am the loyalty

I am not the girl who dances like no one is watching

but I am the consistency

I am not the one who will make you say "how did I get this lucky"

but I am the dutiful

I am not the girl with no troubles, carefree with no baggage

but I am the damaged

I am not the one you were looking for

but I am the one who found you

I am not the beauty that sweeps away

your very breath, before you ever take it

but I am here.

I will never be that girl

but I will be the woman who loves you.

I am only everything you thought you didn't need.

Dandelion, my dandelion

Rain on me your showers of mourning

Allow me to carry the burden that life brings

Share with me, your every short-coming

Don't ever be afraid...

Trust me with your biggest dreams

and know I'll never intend to crush them.

Beautiful dandelion, you sway with the summer winds

you bend so far but never break

I'll do my best, to always take

your every tear and wipe away

This heart you have, will never age

Come, knock on my door, peer through my windows,

climb into my bed, because this world is a bad dream

Trust me baby, I know

But right here, is where I'll always be

Dandelion, my dandelion

you can always count on me.

hues of everlong

Paint the dark night skies

hues of ever longing gray

whispers in the clouds

paint the trees

and paint my stars

paint me in the night sky

paint me as you wave goodbye

paint me in the pouring rain

paint me so you'll remember my face,

even if you never see me again.

you make me want to dance

Dancing freely, you'll find me, while I sit very still.

I'll reminisce of the girl who lived outside of this box...

my brother drew

Restless, so it always seems

it's hard for me to let go

of something that sits so close by

that I never got the chance to know.

You could have been my partner

through all of what became of them

but had you never left us

who knows what would have happened then.

This life would be so different

If I hadn't always been so alone

I needed you more than they did

I could feel it in my bones.

And some nights you'd come to my bedside

and you'd whisper that you love me

but most nights, I'd just turn over

because days without you had gotten ugly.

When I opened birthday boxes

in the middle of december

filled with valentines from last year

even though my birthday's in september

and every time the phone would ring

and she'd be on the other end

telling me inappropriate secrets

and trying to be my friend

she knew that being my mother,

was a concept so long lost

there wasn't much else she could do

but tell me how much I didn't matter

and that the family I'd been given wasn't mine at all.

"he was so young, such a beautiful boy"

To a 10 year old girl, this is what she said

"it should have been you, but he's the one dead"

Years of drug abuse, and pretending we didn't exist

And she would come crying to me

Like it was something I needed to fix.

This mother I was given, you were given her too.

And my father, he's always been just mine

but I would have shared him with you.

Because of all the things I would like to change

I know this to be most true

my life would have been so different

with you, my brother Drew.

So now right there on my shoulders

where your wings probably are

is "wish you were here" forever

and your death date, inked in scars.

How do I explain

that even though the voices in my head insist that this all feels wrong, I know that it's right because
there is literal love oozing from my pores, and I can't hold it back? That even though you may not see
it, I am composed of nothing but ways for me to care for you

I know that when there are too many things happening all at once, I start to feel scattered, like
everything is a chaotic mess, so I sit on the floor and sort out the messes

Until they're organized enough

that my vision stops blurring

and the voices aren't whirring,

and the matchsticks aren't burning in the ocean.

Trying so hard to exist in the positive,

a constant shamble of panic, and anxiety.

Shadow of a doubt is my worst nightmare.

Blindfolded and wandering in an empty field,

searching for the way out,

tripping over disbelief.

My own two feet deceive me.

It's like being alive without ever really living.

It's like being a monster,

But what you don't know, is that I hide from me too.

ocd

Hiding from my own reflection,

screaming something about perfection,

never really reaching my full potential

because I'm tied down by the weight of what I haven't done.

Fragments of ideas,

and ideas about plans,

and plans to do anything,

that never come to be-

because I'm stagnant like the air surrounding,

and hope wreaks of missed opportunity and desperation.

This is what it means,

to be emotionally broken.

Mentally scarred.

It means constantly having to explain who you are.

Not just for reason,

but because your compulsions convince you,

that no matter how many times you've told everyone,

they still don't understand you....

rainboots

Holding my hand on the rainy walk home

skipping, in yellow rain boots too close to the road

falling from the sidewalk, tripping over my own toes

stumbling in between the white dotted lines,

speeding, reckless, right through the stop sign

my monster is chasing me, yelling to get out of the way

but the headlights are on me, as I sit down to play

Piano keys play, the sounds of the rain

It's loud, and I'm quiet, as I'm fighting to inhale

I've no hearing, no feeling, no movement, no vision.

screeches behind me and the pounding heart beyond

for the monster who must keep living, even when I'm gone.

unprecedented bloom

Unfold and widespread like flower buds

expanding your nectars for the hummingbirds to taste

drawing the eye of passerby with the flaming yellow petals

surrounded by uncouth weeds demanding your nutrients

stripped from deep violets you hate.

Birthing color changes, growth flourishes in the spring

enjoy the sunlight before the frost

drink the warmth before it's gone.

the same cloth

Beauty dances in an empty ballroom

it moves barefoot in circles and waves

to the sounds of violins in a distant village.

through the keyhole I peer

the walls adorned in tarnished brass

the claps of beauty's feet as she moves

echoing through my heartbeat

my blood pumps slowly, tingles climb up my spine

my hands reach out to knock

but I know she won't let me in.

The flowers that bloom beneath her feet won't let go

beauty is a lonely blossom, that I can't seem to pick.

Hatred is a windstorm that breathes through your windows

storm shutters torn away, and tossed aside

suffocating beneath the surface

the feeling that you can't hide

grasping for dear life when the doors fly open

and everything is ripped away

fingertips curled onto nothingness

you're gone.

and hatred is screaming in the center of an empty field

falling to it's knees, confused

What was once there, was too much so he removed it

but now he's alone, scouring for a heart that was left behind.

composition

I'm no stranger to

decomposing of everything

you think I might be

wish for sweet somethings

the absence of my nothing

I want to shine, bright

heat

When you're the one on fire

can you feel the heat of the flames?

If I'm burned long enough to remove my identity

can I trace my fingerprints to become the person I've imagined?

If my physical is scorching, does my mental prepare for it or just react?

If I were the fire starter, who would be the water for me?

Should I warrant the waves of cool water splashing away my demise?

Or should I call out only yesterdays, in hopes that someone hears my pleas

and rushes to rescue the weeping whose tears evaporate before they fall bzzz...

Crumble, my little humble bee

Your buzz is just too slight for me.

when I was small

Bleed the fortune of your good nature

into the roots of something bigger

the tree that will grow

and someday she will stand beneath it

and find a place to rest her head

she will look up to the sky

she will ponder what instead

could have come, of so much more

than all of what she never considered

and if the clouds would open up

and show her there is something bigger

than everything she thought she knew

she must know it's too late,

she is free to breathe deeply

inhale particles of your being

exhale pieces of what he used to be

and down she goes

like a ton of bricks...

weighted by guilt and strung out on resilience.

oil slick

Dip your hands into the river of colors

each individual hue will slide from your fingertips

Like an oil slick escaping the rain

Such is the same with every hurt

that refuses to feel

overlooked as it heals, and it heals

stacks of infinite suffering

Piled on top, on top, on top

until the pain falls... comes crashing down around you like a million flesh bound books

and every individual chapter lands directly on your heart

and you feel like you can't breathe, like this will be what tears you apart

until you learn how to dodge it, you skip the chapters that break you

you turn the pages as the stories fly by, so swiftly your hair whips around you

you reach out to catch them, to analyze and interpret, to pinpoint that one word, the sentence that must have done it...

but the paper slices your fingers as it whirls in the opposite direction

and you stand up to chase it, but you realize your feet are planting you in this upright position

but they refuse to move, you're stuck still- forced to simply watch.

You don't know how to change it, how to accommodate, to adjust...

You just know how to be the you that all of this taught you to be. Still.

Still me, still my story, still my suffering, still my pain.

Still going to be me, no matter how much I wish it all away.

feeling

Head to toe encompassed in absolute feeling

Here I stand ignorant; yet aware- in the center of a town made entirely of glass

I rest well, completely in control, for every direction I glance there is all to see

and all of what happens beyond my glass walls cannot directly affect me.

I sit at the base of the wall with no beginning and no end, searching for proof of divine anything

beyond intervention, but simply solace in the understanding that my barrier protects yet confines me

To be safe is to be blind, and to open your eyes is a waste of time if you seek not the answers of truth.

what does any of this even mean?

My surroundings speak to me with whispers through the cracks in the walls

every patch of missing paint is a fracture to my multitude-

of all the things I should be feeling

I open my eyes with my physical being

but hollowness consumes me in a place that no one else can see.

The creature inside of me scratches at the back of my tongue

never allowing me to say everything I need to say

to get it off my chest and into YOUR head

to fester

and force ponder... in a way that makes you want to claw at your ears until they bleed

only to realize you've enforced your own suffering.

Is this what dying feels like?

There is a far-off melody conducting the soundtrack

to the downfall of who I've tried to be.

I try to hum along but I'm completely out of breath.

Gasping,

reaching,

Defeated,

As I'm composing the symphony of what feels like my own death.

collapsing

My chest is heavy, I'm not breathing,

but I can so clearly visualize you and me-standing in a field of color,

dancing wild as we paint the stars into the night sky

My lungs are collapsing, But I can feel the tips of your fingers tracing my suffocation

My veins are pulsing, beating every bit of me through the depths of what you've done

I spin around the symptoms of madness, in a world that used to stand still for you

My foundation is cracking, the seams to everything I believed are splitting

All of me, where did she go?

What have you done...?

Why did you think...?

What happened when...?

Hard pressed to voice his guilt, is the man that destroyed my world in a series of instances...

None of which included me.

flinch

Hold still, don't move an inch.

Don't flinch, don't scream

just tell yourself it's all a dream.

Spontaneous combustion

Fragile mental matter

Years of hardship arranged on a silver platter.

Hold still, show me how you lead the life you do

bliss achieved only through ignorance

air stagnant, breathing in fragments

entirely composed of another being

Lead your own life, control your fate

It's never too late to change your pace.

Never fear letting go, and never fear what fear consumes.

Let go of your pride for just a moment, and you'll be surprised what you can do.

happy pills

Choke the last of every meaningful

word I have, right out of me.

Strangle me senseless,

and question my sanity.

Shun my intelligence,

because you don't have any.

Fuck you, your doubt, your shame.

Fuck everything you've ever said to me.

I can hardly breathe, gagging on your ego.

Holier than thou, and not a god damn thing to show for it.

you are enough

You are more than enough

to prioritize yourself

never take the backseat

To someone whose only interest

is to strip you of everything that you are

Human nature

Pay close attention

to the nature of an abuser

It's not their fault

It never is

It's always yours

You did ALL OF THIS

And while you're down there

You're ugly

You're stupid

Get out of the way

And don't forget

It's your own fault

That they're acting this way

that's not true

How can I believe any of what you say?

If I know that you only act in spite of me?

And in this moment

I am exactly where I belong

I'm doing everything that I need to

I'm making my own choices

And I'm suffering my own consequences

I'm figuring it out

One band aid at a time